Life and Other Options

Reflections for the Curious, Bewildered, Weary, Frustrated and Skeptical

Compiled and Edited by
ANITA BERGEN

Life and Other Options
Anita Bergen

Published in the United States of America
New World Publishing
Atlanta, GA 30102

New World Publishing
March, 2014

ISBN   9 780943 477343

For "the boys":
Scott and his big brother

Foreword

by John Harricharan

I've always believed that the ability to make choices was a special gift from our Creator. When Anita Bergen first told me about *Life and Other Options* my initial reaction was there could be no other option to life, that life either *is* or *isn't*. Yet, in retrospect, it would seem that there are several options in life, options such as to live life gloriously and to its fullest, to use the abilities and gifts we came here with, to leave this place a little better than we found it, to make a difference.

Other options would be to live life at the bottom of the barrel, to eke out a meager existence and to plod a weary, whining way from birth to death. Yes, as in almost everything, there are options as to how life could be lived.

I have traveled a strange path to this point in life. From my birth in a little farming village to my current occupation as an author and lecturer, I've seen the best and the worst of humanity. I've mourned the death of my wife, wept at the passing of my parents and grieved at the graveside of some of my best friends. I've climbed the heights of happiness, descended into depths of despair and have visited many points between those two extremes. And still, I wonder how I made it through to this day.

I am here, precisely because others have paved the way for me. The great minds of history have left gifts of wisdom to guide us through the most treacherous rapids on the river of life.

They have given us a rich legacy encapsulated in words, handed down from one generation to the next. Modern day guides and teachers leave us books to read to help us or entertain us on our journey. But alas! Today there seems to be no time to even touch the tip of this monumental collection of the earth's wisdom. We hunt and peck, hoping that we may uncover some gems of wisdom to help us along. We long for a helping hand to point the way.

I was thrilled to find *Life and Other Options*. Anita Bergen has compiled a marvelous anthology of the best this world has to offer. This is not a book of quotations like other quotation books I've seen. This is a well thought out volume, which captures the essence of humanity and, at the same time, serves as a map through the mazes of life. Anita has collected the very thoughts that sustained me through some of the lowest moments of my life. She has, in fact, provided us with a book of magic, a book that spans time and space to bring us the very words we need when the tempests roar all around us.

I have used the quotes Anita has compiled to help make a point during many of my lectures. They have been with me as a comfort when I faced the cold, hard winds of life. They have shown me a way when there appeared to be no way at all. They have comforted me, brought tears to my eyes, moved me to the mountaintop and provided a helping hand. You, too, will find strength in these pages. You will find the courage, hope and faith to keep on keeping on until you finally break through your limitations into the sunlight of success.

Thank you, Anita, for making it possible for us to have *Life and Other Options*. Some of these quotes will comfort, guide and tweak our conscience while others may even provoke us. However, all will cause us to think and feel. I look forward to your other volumes, which will continue the fine tradition you have so bravely begun. As for myself, I choose life—life as it was meant to be, life in all its glory, joys, sadness, grief, pain, success, failure, triumph and bliss. Thank you, also, for the privilege of sharing these few words with your readers. You've lit a lamp, which in time will lighten the hearts of many.

Atlanta, Georgia

Introduction

The truth is that life is hard and dangerous;
that he who seeks his own happiness does not
find it;
that he who is weak must suffer;
that he who demands love, will be disappointed;
that he who is greedy, will not be fed;
that he who seeks peace, will find strife;
that truth is only for the brave;
that joy is only for him who does not fear to be
alone;
that life is only for the one who is not afraid to die.
— Joyce Carey

Joyce Carey's expressive quote says it all: "The
truth is that life is hard and dangerous."

That, I discovered, is the trouble with truth. Truth
is elegant, simple, always eloquent and most times
as exasperating as it is disturbing. Truth is as
abundant as air and is everywhere around us. Yet,
like air, it is taken for granted and often just as
difficult to grasp. Even the most elegantly simple
truth can be compared to a double-edged sword. It
always presents major challenges.

The first challenge is in the search for truth itself. Most times the discovery of truth occurs "by accident." We're more likely to trip over it or stumble upon it than to find it as the result of deliberate search—more or less, a discovery "by accident." Today very few of us have the time or resources to set off on a deliberate quest to unearth the grail of truth. What we're really after is a fix for our current problem or dilemma.

Some say discovery "by accident" is a phenomenon that may be attributed to many causes, among them: synergy, luck, serendipity or just plain "being in the right place at the right time." Others believe that there are no accidents. The ancient injunction urges us to ask and you will receive; seek and you will find; knock and it will be opened unto you.

Through many dark, troubling hours of the soul I've felt great comfort after stumbling upon an inspiring reflection "by accident." There's tremendous consolation just knowing that others have survived and even conquered the same ordeal. By looking in the right place—perhaps, this book—we might encourage an "accidental discovery."

While discovering truth is important, being aware that the solution to our problem exists is only half the answer. The second and far more difficult challenge is in using our newly discovered truth as a tool for fixing the problem. Now we must put this truth to use, applying it to the problem so the solution may occur.

It takes relatively few encounters with reality to turn a normally cheerful optimist into a cynical skeptic, wasting on the doorstep of despair. A new millennium, nevertheless, has dawned on an old world—a world of dualities. One world we inherit, complete with a legacy of conflict, insensitivity and greed. The other world will be a child of our own creation.

We long for a safe, nurturing environment—one where we can work toward reaching our potential, solving our problems and fulfilling our dreams. Yet our world has become so competitive, insensitive and commercial that many struggle to survive without being engulfed by anxiety, stress, deception, disappointment, loss and betrayal.

And that's just it. At the end of the day, even if we win the battle, we're still sick and tired of merely surviving and losing the war. Our soul aches to live life joyously, to soar free above the ordinary.

Of course, we haven't been singled out; our experience isn't unique. What we are feeling, the emotions we're struggling with and the difficulties we're wrestling to subdue have all been encountered before. Many experienced, knowledgeable seekers have also traveled this path. An old Chinese proverb states: "To know the road ahead, ask those coming back."

"That's precisely what I need to do;" you might reason, "get some solutions from those who have been there. But where can I find these 'old souls'?"

In *Life and Other Options* I've put together a collection of inspiring, insightful reflections spoken by some of the greatest 'old souls' the world has ever known. These quotations have been gathered from the great spiritual teachers of all religious traditions, ancient and modern, both Eastern and Western. It also includes excerpts from playwrights, poets, authors, philosophers, psychologists, athletes, entertainers and heads of state, both past and present.

I've designed *Life and Other Options* to be used as a personal, inspirational guidance tool. Keep it handy where you can reach it: open, if you like, on the coffee table, within arm's reach by your desk, or on your nightstand, if you prefer. At any time, just open it to any page and you are sure to find a meaningful, relevant message.

Life and Other Options was created to assist you in making your own discoveries "by accident." It's not that discovering someone else's insight will automatically solve our problems. Throughout life we never cease meeting obstacles. If we use a map, however, we're better prepared to venture into unfamiliar territory.

The burdens don't cease to appear; but we learn to develop patience and stronger spiritual muscles so the burdens aren't nearly as heavy. We don't need to re-invent the wheel. The best way to find the answers we seek is to observe another's experience, to wait in quiet expectation and listen for guidance.

There are times in some of our most difficult personal conflicts and tragedies when life seems to lose its meaning. We lose our way when we most need to hear the few inspiring words that would urge us on. Toward this end, perhaps, this anthology may serve its purpose of inspiration and renewal.

Creating this book has been a tremendously inspiring and rewarding experience, not only intellectually, but emotionally and spiritually as well. It is my sincere hope that *Life and Other Options* will prove helpful in furnishing some light and insight on the enigma we experience as life.

For with all its unanswered questions, life still manages to offer an infinite number of options.
Our only job, the sages remind us, is to make choices.

Anita Bergen

Choice! The key is choice. You have options. You need not spend your life wallowing in failure, ignorance, grief, poverty, shame, and self-pity. But, hold on! If this is true why have so many among us apparently elected to live in that manner?

The answer is obvious. Those who live in unhappy failure have never exercised their options for a better way of life because they have never been aware that they had any choices!
— Og Mandino

The search for static security is misguided. Security can only be achieved through adapting old ideas to current facts. Life is under no obligation to give us what we expect, and expecting the world to treat you fairly because you are a good person is like expecting a bull not to charge you because you are a vegetarian.
— Alex Sanders

Life is lived from within and one can never be hurt by what appears to be happening outside. You can change circumstances if you so desire. Your only purpose in life is to make choices. Once the choice is made, the entire universe moves to bring into fruition that which you choose.
— John Harricharan

Sometimes we turn to God when our foundations are shaking only to find out it is God who is shaking them.
— Unknown

The first rule of holes: when you're in one, stop digging.
— Molly Ivins

Five Simple Rules to Follow to Live a Happy Life:

1. Free your heart from hatred.
2. Free your mind from worries.
3. Live simply.
4. Give more.
5. Expect Less.

No one can go back and make a brand new start. Anyone can start from now and make a brand new ending. Life didn't promise days without pain, laughter without sorrow, sun without rain, but it did promise strength for the day, comfort for the tears, and light for the way.
— Unknown

If you don't like how things are, change it! You're not a tree. You have the ability to totally transform every area in your life — and it all begins with your very own power of choice.
— Jim Rohn

Life isn't about keeping score. It's not about how many people call you and it's not about whom you've dated, are dating or haven't dated at all. It isn't about whom you've kissed, what sport you play, or which guy or girl likes you. It's not about your shoes or your hair or the color of your skin or where you live or go to school. In fact, it's not about grades, money, clothes, or colleges that accept you or not. Life isn't about if you have lots of friends, or if you are alone, and it's not about how accepted or unaccepted you are. Life just isn't about that.

But life is about whom you love and whom you hurt. It's about how you feel about yourself. It's about trust, happiness, and compassion. It's about sticking up for your friends and replacing inner hate with love. Life is about avoiding jealousy, overcoming ignorance and building confidence. It's about what you say and what you mean. It's about seeing people for who they are and not what they have. Most of all, it is about choosing to use your life to touch someone else's in a way that could never have been achieved otherwise. These choices are what life is about.
— Unknown

It is our choices that show what we truly are, far more than our abilities.
— J. K. Rowling

We are the choices we have made.
— Meryl Streep

Life is the sum of all your choices.
— Albert Camus

Anita Bergen

People are always blaming their circumstances
for what they are. I don't believe in
circumstances. The people who get on in this
world are the people who get up and look for the
circumstances they want and, if they can't find
them, make them.
— George Bernard Shaw

If one advances confidently in the direction of his
dreams, and endeavors to live the life which he
has imagined, he will meet with a success
unexpected in common hours. . . Why should we
be in such desperate haste to succeed, and in
such desperate enterprises? If a man does not
keep pace with his companions, perhaps it is
because he hears a different drummer. Let him
step to the music which he hears, however
measured or far away.
— Henry David Thoreau

The Golden Rule: Do unto others as you would have them do unto you.

The Silver Rule: Do for yourself at least as much as you do for others.

The Iron Rule: Don't do for others what they can do for themselves.
— Unknown

>⟶⟶

You may believe that you are responsible for what you do, but not for what you think. The truth is that you are responsible for what you think, because it is only at this level that you can exercise choice. What you do comes from what you think.
— A Course in Miracles

>⟶⟶

The key to happiness is having dreams.
The key to success is making dreams come true.
—Unknown

Life is neither the candle nor the wick;
it is the burning.
—Unknown

Life is:
Life is an opportunity, benefit from it.
Life is beauty, admire it.
Life is bliss, taste it.
Life is a dream, realize it.
Life is a challenge, meet it.
Life is a duty, complete it.
Life is a game, play it.
Life is a promise, fulfill it.
Life is sorrow, overcome it.
Life is a song, sing it.
Life is a struggle, accept it.
Life is a tragedy, confront it.
Life is an adventure, dare it.
Life is luck, make it.
Life is too precious; do not destroy it.
Life is life, fight for it.
— Mother Teresa

In your hands will be placed the exact results of your thoughts; you will receive that which you earn, no more, no less. Whatever your present environment may be, you will fail, remain, or rise with your thoughts, your wisdom, desire, as great as your dominant aspiration.
— James Allen

All people dream, but not equally.
Those who dream by night in the dusty recesses of their mind, wake in the morning to find that it was vanity.

But the dreamers of the day are dangerous people, for they dream their dreams with open eyes, and make them come true.
— T.E. Lawrence, a.k.a. Lawrence of Arabia

A visionary is one who can find his way by moonlight, and see the dawn before the rest of the world.
— Oscar Wilde

9

To be yourself in a world that is constantly trying to make you something else is the greatest accomplishment.
— Ralph Waldo Emerson

The more faithfully you listen to the voice within you, the better you will hear what is sounding outside. And only he who listens can speak.
— Dag Hammerskjöld

I found I had less and less to say, until finally, I became silent, and began to listen. I discovered in the silence, the voice of God.
— Søren Kierkegaard

One is always considered mad, when one discovers something that others cannot grasp.
— Edward D. Wood

And I said to the man who stood at the gate of the year, "Give me a light that I may tread safely into the unknown."

And he replied, "Go out into the darkness and put your hand into the hand of God. That shall be to you better than light and safer than a known way."
— Louise Haskins

><del></del>

"Come to the edge," he said.

They said, "We are afraid."

"Come to the edge," he said.
They came. He pushed them ...
And they flew.
— Guillaume Apollinaire

><del></del>

A man may fall many times but he won't be a failure until he says someone pushed him.
— Elmer G. Letterman

11

The greater danger for most of us is not that our aim is too high and we miss it, but that it is too low and we reach it.
— Michelangelo Buonarroti

＞￢￢

Champions aren't made in the gyms. Champions are made from something they have deep inside them—a desire, a dream,
a vision.
— Muhammad Ali

＞￢￢

The best thing in life is doing things people say you can't do.
— Jennifer Moore

All blame is a waste of time. No matter how much fault you find with another, and regardless of how much you blame him, it will not change you. The only thing blame does is to keep the focus off you when you are looking for external reasons to explain your unhappiness or frustration. You may succeed in making another feel guilty about something by blaming him, but you won't succeed in changing whatever it is about you that is making you unhappy.
— Wayne Dyer

Great spirits have always encountered violent opposition from mediocre minds.
— Albert Einstein

This is the true joy in life, the being used for a purpose recognized by yourself as a mighty one; the being thoroughly worn out before you are thrown on the scrap heap; the being a force of nature instead of a feverish, selfish little clod of ailments and grievances complaining that the world will not devote itself to making you happy.
— George Bernard Shaw

13

There is no such thing as a problem without a
gift for you in its hands.
You seek problems because you need their gifts.
— Richard Bach

For every problem, there is a solution, which is
simple, neat and wrong.
— H. L. Mencken

Just two things are necessary for success in this
life:
One is a sense of purpose and the other is a
touch of madness.
— John Harricharan

The indispensable first step to getting the things
you want out of life is this:
Decide what you want.
— Ben Stein

Seek out that particular mental attribute which makes you feel most deeply and vitally alive, along with which comes the inner voice which says, "This is the real me," and when you have found that attitude, follow it.
— William James

You will not grow if you sit in a beautiful flower garden, but you will grow if you are sick, if you are in pain, if you experience losses, and if you do not put your head in the sand. Take the pain as a gift to you with a very, very specific purpose.
— Elisabeth Kübler-Ross

Accept the pain, cherish the joys, resolve the regrets; then can come the best of benedictions: "If I had my life to live over, I'd do it all the same."
— Joan McIntosh

In the quiet of this day may you know the
greatness of your spirit and may your hopes fly
on the wings of possibility.
— Mary Anne Radmacher

Challenge

Sometimes we have to walk
'close to the edge'.
Sometimes our dreams demand it.
Whether that walk speaks of
courage or foolishness —
Something inside
Just commands it!
Living in fear is
NOT where I am.
There's so much to do
In this life.

I'll stand to be counted
Among those who care;
And not consciously figure the price.
— Jeni Prigmore

Now is the only time there is. Make your now wow, your minutes miracles, and your days pay. Your life will have been magnificently lived and invested, and when you die you will have made a difference.
— Mark Victor Hansen

Be faithful to that which exists nowhere but in yourself—and thus make yourself indispensable.
— André Gide

The biggest mistake people make in life is not trying to make a living at doing what they most enjoy.
— Malcolm Forbes

Use the talents you possess—for the woods would be silent if no birds sang but the best.
— Henry Jackson van Dyke

The great Western disease is, 'I'll be happy
when... When I get the money.
When I get a BMW. When I get this job.' Well, the
reality is, you never get to when. The only way to
find happiness is to understand that happiness
is not out there. It's in here. And happiness is
not next week. It's now.
— Marshall Goldsmith

Start living now. Stop saving the good china for
that special occasion. Stop withholding your love
until that special person materializes.

Every day you are alive is a special occasion.
Every minute, every breath,
is a gift from God.
— Mary Manin Morrissey

Seize the moment. Remember all those women
on the Titanic who waved off the dessert cart.
— Erma Bombeck

When you are clear about what you want to
learn, you will find your teacher. The teacher is
already there. The two of you will meet because
you are looking for each other.
— W.A. Mathieu

What is a good man but a bad man's teacher?

What is a bad man but a good man's job?

If you don't understand this, you will get lost,
however intelligent you are.

It is the great secret.
— Lao-tzu

The thing always happens that you really believe
in; and the belief in a thing makes it happen.
— Frank Lloyd Wright

One day Alice came to a fork in the road and saw a Cheshire Cat in a tree.

"Would you tell me, please, which way I ought to go from here?"

"That depends a good deal on where you want to get to," said the Cheshire Cat.
"I don't much care where" said Alice.

"Then it doesn't matter which way you go," said the Cat.

"--so long as I get SOMEWHERE," Alice added as an explanation.

"Oh, you're sure to do that," said the Cat, "if you only walk long enough."
— Lewis Carroll, *Alice's Adventures in Wonderland*

>m~

In a world gone mad with illusion, a touch of madness is the only sanity.
— Robert "Butch" James

"What sort of people live about here?"

"In that direction," the Cat said, waving its right paw round, "lives a Hatter: and in that direction," waving the other paw, "lives a March Hare. Visit either you like: they're both mad."

"But I don't want to go among mad people," Alice remarked.

"Oh, you can't help that," said the Cat: "we're all mad here. I'm mad. You're mad."

"How do you know I'm mad?" said Alice.

"You must be," said the Cat, "or you wouldn't have come here."
— Lewis Carroll, *Alice's Adventures in Wonderland*

>⟶~

When we remember we are all mad, the mysteries disappear and life stands explained.
— Mark Twain

21

Nothing is as real as a dream. The world can change around you, but your dream will not. Responsibilities need not erase it. Duties need not obscure it. Because the dream is within you, no one can take it away.
— Tom Clancy

The world would have you agree with its dismal dream of limitation. But the light would have you soar like the eagle of your sacred visions.
— Alan Cohen

If a man wishes to be sure of the road he treads on, he must close his eyes and walk in the dark.
— St. John of the Cross

Do you want me to tell you something really subversive? Love is everything it's cracked up to be. That's why people are so cynical about it. It really is worth fighting for, being brave for, risking everything for. And the trouble is, if you don't risk anything, you risk even more.
— Erica Jong

There are only four questions of value in life, Don Octavio:

What is sacred?
Of what is the spirit made?
What is worth living for,
and what is worth dying for?

The answer to each is the same: only love.
— Don Juan (Johnny Depp),
Don Juan de Marco

There is only one happiness in life,
to love and be loved.
— George Sand

When you get to the end of all the light you know
and it's time to step into the darkness of the
unknown, faith is knowing that one of two things
shall happen: either you will be given something
solid to stand on, or you will be taught how to
fly.
— Edward Teller

>⟊⟊

Find Purpose....the means shall follow.
— Mahatma Gandhi

>⟊⟊

Your body is the ground and metaphor of your
life, the expression of your existence. It is your
Bible, your encyclopedia, your life story.
Everything that happens to you is stored and
reflected in your body.
 In the marriage of flesh and spirit divorce is
impossible.
— Gabrielle Roth

24

An ancient said, "When confusion ceases, tranquility comes; when tranquility comes, wisdom appears, and when wisdom appears, reality is seen.
— Keizan Jokan

Reality is an illusion.
— Anita Bergen

Reality is something you rise above.
— Liza Minelli

Change is created by those whose imaginations are bigger than their circumstances.
— Unknown

I have had a long life full of troubles,
but there is one curious fact about them—nine-
tenths of them never happened.
— Andrew Carnegie

If you don't learn to laugh at troubles, you won't
have anything to laugh at when you grow old.
— Edward W. Howe

The greater part of our happiness or misery
depends on our dispositions and not on our
circumstances.
— Martha Washington

We who lived in concentration camps can remember the men who walked through the huts comforting others, giving away their last piece of bread. They may have been few in number, but they offer sufficient proof that everything can be taken from a man but one thing: the last of the human freedoms—to choose one's attitude in any given set of circumstances, to choose one's own way.
— Victor Frankl

I believe in the sun even though it is slow in rising. I believe in you without realizing. I believe in rain though there are no clouds in the sky. I believe in truth even though people lie. I believe in peace though sometimes I am violent. I believe in God even though he is silent.
— Unknown

I will love the light for it shows me the way. Yet I will endure the darkness for it shows me the stars.
— Og Mandino

The aim of life is to live, and to live means to be aware, joyously, drunkenly, serenely, divinely aware.
— Henry Miller

Life is not a journey to the grave with the intention of arriving safely in a pretty and well preserved body, but rather to skid in sideways, thoroughly used up, totally worn out, and loudly proclaiming, "Wow - what a Ride!"
— Peter Sage

. . . the universe gives to those who plug in, mediocrity is self-inflicted and genius is self-bestowed. We should cultivate the silence, and when we are alone, the universe will talk to us in flashes of inspiration.
— Eric Butterworth

If you cannot find the truth right where you are, where else do you expect to find it?
— Dogen

Speak the truth wherever you may find it. Seek the truth wherever it is to be found. Don't confuse facts with truth. Facts may not even be facts at all. Most times, they're just opinions. Facts are relative. Truth is absolute. Instead of trying to force your facts on others, help them to find truth for themselves.
— John Harricharan

The truth is more important than the facts.
— Frank Lloyd Wright

The truth will set you free, but first it will make you miserable.
— James A. Garfield

When you blame others, you give up your power to change.
— Dr. Robert Anthony

Silence is the great teacher, and to learn its lessons you must pay attention to it. There is no substitute for the creative inspiration, knowledge, and stability that comes from knowing how to contact your core of inner silence.
— Deepak Chopra

The only thing that makes life possible is permanent, intolerable uncertainty: not knowing what comes next.
— Ursula K. LeGuin

Your own body is not your possession. It is the shape lent to you by heaven and earth. Your life is not your possession; it is harmony between your forces, granted for a time by heaven and earth. Your nature and destiny are not your possessions; they are the course laid down for you by heaven and earth. Your children and grandchildren are not your possessions; heaven and earth lend them to you to cast off from your body as an insect sheds its skin. Therefore you travel without knowing where you go, stay without knowing what you cling to, are fed without knowing how. You are the breath of heaven and earth, which goes to and fro; how can you ever possess it?
— Lieh-Tzu

To attain knowledge, add things every day.
To attain wisdom, remove things every day.
— Lao Tzu

Regret is an appalling waste of energy; you can't build on it; it is good only for wallowing in.
— Katherine Mansfield

There are three kinds of people and three kinds of richness:
— people who want to have, to collect
— people who want action, work and labor
— people who want to be

The real richness is in be-ness. People can take all that you have, all that you collected. People can stop your labor, or an accident can stop you. When you are, you never lose what you are.
— Torkom Saraydarian

Ⓘ

The Best Thing to Give:

The best thing to give your enemy is forgiveness
To an opponent, tolerance
To a friend, your heart
To your child, a good example
To a father, deference
To your mother, conduct that will make her proud of you
To yourself, respect
To all men, charity
— Unknown

32

Men have been taught that it is a virtue to agree with others.
But the creator is the man who disagrees.
Men have been taught that it is a virtue to swim with the current.
But the creator is the man who goes against the current.
Men have been taught that it is a virtue to stand together.
But the creator is the man who stands alone.
— Ayn Rand

The only job we have been given when we came to this earth is to create. Everything we do is a creation, from a job, to children to thoughts. We all create all the time; it is all we do.
— Tom Justin

When the gods wish to punish us, they answer our prayers.
— Oscar Wilde

33

Every person is endowed with the inalienable
right to clothe his God in the essence of his
unique imagination.
— Rick Prigmore

꙳

Religion is for people who are afraid of going to
hell; spirituality is for those who have been
there.
— member of Alcoholics Anonymous

꙳

Men may be divided almost any way we please,
but I have found the most useful distinction to
be made between those who devote their lives to
conjugating the verb 'to be', and those who
spend their lives conjugating the verb 'to have.'
— Sydney J. Harris

A man's true wealth is the good he does in this
world.
— Mohammed

There is no need to run outside
For better seeing . . .
Rather abide
At the center of your being;
For the more you leave it, the less you learn.
Search your heart and see . . .
The way to do is to be.
— Lao-tzu

I am always with all beings;
I abandon no one. And
however great your inner darkness,
you are never separate from me.

Let your thoughts flow past you, calmly;
keep me near, at every moment;
trust me with your life, because I
am you, more than you yourself are.
— Bhagavad Gita

35

Courage is the capacity to go from failure to
failure without losing enthusiasm.
— Winston Churchill

Courage looks you straight in the eye. She is not
impressed with power trippers, and she knows
first aid. Courage is not afraid to weep, and she
is not afraid to pray, even when she is not sure
who she is praying to. When she walks it is clear
she has made the journey from lonliness to
solitude. The people who told me she was stern
were not lying; they just forgot to mention she
was kind.
— J. Ruth Gendler

Courage is the price that life exacts for granting
peace.
— Amelia Earhart

When you aim for perfection, you discover it's a moving target.
— George Fisher

The Problem with Perfection —

Perfection does not exist.
To understand this is the triumph of human intelligence; to expect to possess it is the most dangerous kind of madness.
— Alfred De Musset

Life is eternal, and love is immortal; and death is only a horizon; and a horizon is nothing save the limit of our sight.
— Unknown

There is a vitality, a life force, an energy, a
quickening, that is translated through you into
action, and because there is only one of you in
all time, this expression is unique.
— Martha Graham

Recognize that you are unique in all eternity...
You are one of a kind ! ...there is nobody like
you anywhere on Earth today, and there never
will be anybody like you in all eternity, because
the Universe never duplicates itself. It all boils
down to the fact that if any one of us does not
fulfill that purpose for which he or she was
placed on Earth, growth is slowed down because
nobody can do what you do, exactly the way you
do it.

Very simply, that means that there is no
competition.
— Foster Hibbard

In this world there are only two tragedies.

One is not getting what one wants,
and the other is getting it.
— Oscar Wilde

The happiest people are those who think the
most interesting thoughts. Those who decide to
use leisure as a means of mental development,
who love good music, good books, good pictures,
good company, good conversation, are the
happiest people in the world. And they are not
only happy in themselves, they are the cause of
happiness in others.
— William Lyon Phelps

Look carefully at the closest associations in your
life, for that is the direction you are heading.
— Unknown

Begin doing what you want to do now.
We are not living in eternity. We have only this
moment, sparkling like a star in our hand and
melting like a snowflake.
— Marie Beyon Ray

Life is easier than you'd think;
all that is necessary is to accept
the impossible, do without the indispensable,
and bear the intolerable.
— Kathleen Norris

We live in a world of theophanies. Holiness
comes wrapped in the ordinary. There are
burning bushes all around you. Every tree is full
of angels. Hidden beauty is waiting in every
crumb. Life wants to lead you from crumbs to
angels, but this can happen only if you are
willing to unwrap the ordinary by staying with it
long enough to harvest its treasure.
— Macrina Wiederkehr

Justice alone, fundamental as it is, will seldom kindle holiness in a soul in which the light of love is quenched, or burns but dimly. It is justice illumined with mercy that floods the world with ineffable goodness and grace.
— Talmud

Never let your sense of morals get in the way of doing what's right.
— Isaac Asimov

God is like a mirror. The mirror never changes but everybody who looks at it sees something different.
— Rabbi Harold Kushner

Do It Anyway

People are often unreasonable, irrational, and
self-centered; Forgive them anyway.
If you are kind, people may accuse you of selfish,
ulterior motives; Be kind anyway.
If you are successful, you will win some
unfaithful friends and some genuine enemies;
Succeed anyway.

If you are honest and sincere, people may
deceive you; Be honest and sincere anyway.
What you spend years creating, others could
destroy overnight; Create anyway.

If you find serenity and happiness, some may be
jealous; Be happy anyway.
The good you do today, will often be forgotten
tomorrow; Do good anyway.

Give the world the best you have, and it will
never be enough; Give the world your best
anyway.

You see, in the final analysis, it is between you
and God. It was never between you and them
any way.
— Mother Teresa

This is the beginning of a new day.

God has given me this day to use as I will.
I can waste it—or use it for good, but what I do
today is important, because I am exchanging a
day of my life for it!

When tomorrow comes, this day will be gone
forever, leaving in its place something that I have
traded for it.

I want it to be gain, and not loss; good, and not
evil; success, and not failure; in order that I shall
not regret the price I have paid for it.
— Unknown

Your hardest job in life is to survive your well-
meaning birth family. If you can accomplish this,
everything else is a piece of cake.
— Anita Bergen

There are only two ways of getting on in the
world: by one's own industry, or by the stupidity
of others.
— Jean de La Bruyère

You gave your life to become the person you are right now.

Was it worth it?
— Richard Bach

There is only one success—to be able to spend your life in your own way.
— Christopher Morley

You have been told that, even like a chain, you are as weak as your weakest link.

This is but half the truth.
You are also as strong as your strongest link.

To measure you by your smallest deed is to reckon the power of the ocean by the frailty of its foam.
— Kahlil Gibran

I always had a dream that when I am asked to give an accounting of my life to a higher court, it will go like this:
'So, empty your pockets.

What have you got left of your life? Any dreams that were unfulfilled? Any unused talent that we gave you when you were born that you still have left? Any unsaid compliments or bits of love that you haven't spread around?'

And I will answer, 'I've nothing to return.
I spent everything you gave me.
I'm as naked as the day I was born.'

What we do with the talent we're given is all that matters.
— Erma Bombeck

The service we render to others is really the rent we pay for our room on this earth. It is obvious that man is himself a traveler; that the purpose of this world is not 'to have and to hold' but 'to give and to serve.' There can be no other meaning.
— Wilfred T. Grenfell

Life is difficult.

This is a great truth, one of the greatest truths. It is a great truth because once we truly see this truth, we transcend it. Once we truly know that life is difficult—once we truly understand and accept it—then life is no longer difficult. Because once it is accepted, the fact that life is difficult no longer matters.
— M. Scott Peck

The story of a love is not important—what is important is that one is capable of love. It is perhaps the only glimpse we are permitted of eternity.
— Helen Hayes

If one is lucky, a solitary fantasy can totally transform one million realities.
— Maya Angelou

How life catches up with us and teaches us to love and forgive each other.
— Judy Collins

The day will come when, after harnessing the ether, the winds, the tides and gravitation—after all the scientific and technical achievements, we shall harness for God the energies of love. And then, on that day, for the second time in the history of the world, man will have discovered fire!
— Pierre Teilhard de Chardin

The best portion of a good man's life: His little, nameless, unremembered acts of kindness and love.
— William Wordsworth

Whoever undertakes to set himself up as a judge of Truth and Knowledge is shipwrecked by the laughter of the gods.
— Albert Einstein

When an ordinary man attains knowledge, he is a sage; when a sage attains understanding, he is an ordinary man.
— Zen Saying

47

No man can climb out beyond the limitations of
his own character.
— Viscount John Morley

No one does anything uncharacteristic of
who they are.
— Richard Bach

The world we have created is a product of our
thinking. It cannot be changed without changing
our thinking.
— Albert Einstein

Hope is not the conviction that something will
turn out well, but the certainty that something
makes sense, regardless of how it turns out.
— Vaclav Havel

I wanted a perfect ending . . . Now I've learned, the hard way, that some poems don't rhyme, and some stories don't have a clear beginning, middle and end. Life is about not knowing, having to change, taking the moment and making the best of it, without knowing what's going to happen next. Delicious ambiguity.
— Gilda Radner

Life can only be understood backwards; it has to be lived forwards.
— Søren Kierkegaard

One man gets nothing but discord out of a piano; another gets harmony. No one claims the piano is at fault. Life is about the same. The discord is there. Study to play it correctly, and it will give forth the beauty; play it falsely, and it will give forth the ugliness. Life is not at fault.
— Unknown

49

Nothing is worth doing unless the consequences may be serious.
— George Bernard Shaw

When you call upon a thoroughbred, he gives you all the speed, strength of heart and sinew in him. When you call on a jackass, he kicks.
— Patricia Neal, regarding a motto above her father's desk.

We are not human beings trying to be spiritual. We are spiritual beings trying to be human.
— Jacquelyn Small

God made the world round so we would never be able to see too far down the road.
— Isak Dinesen

The weak can never forgive. Forgiveness is the attribute of the strong.
— Mahatma Gandhi

I believe . . . that living on the edge, living in and through your fear, is the summit of life, and that people who refuse to take that dare condemn themselves to a life of living death.
— John H. Johnson

I gain strength, courage and confidence by every experience in which I must stop and look fear in the face. . . I say to myself, I've lived through this and can take the next thing that comes along . . . We must do the things we think we cannot do.
— Eleanor Roosevelt

51

Unawareness is the root of all evil.
— Anonymous Egyptian Monk

There is no difficulty that enough love will not
conquer; no disease that enough love will not
heal; no door that enough love will not open... It
makes no difference how deeply seated may be
the trouble; how hopeless the outlook; how
muddled the tangle; how great the mistake. A
sufficient realization of love will dissolve it all. If
only you could love enough you would be the
happiest and most powerful being in the world.
— Emmet Fox

For one human being to love another: that is
perhaps the most difficult of all our tasks, the
ultimate, the last test and proof, the work for
which all other work is but preparation.
— Rainer Maria Rilke

I think that wherever your journey takes you, there are new gods waiting there, with divine patience—and laughter.
— Susan M. Watkins

Spirituality is a kind of virgin wisdom, a knowing that comes prior to experience.
— Marilyn Ferguson

Trust your hunches. They're usually based on facts filed away just below the conscious level.
— Dr. Joyce Brothers

The more faithfully you listen to the voice within you, the better you will hear what is sounding outside. And only he who listens can speak.
— Dag Hammerskjöld

The universe is full of magical things patiently
waiting for our wits to grow sharper.
— Eden Phillpotts

>᠆᠆

That which makes the tongue speak,
but which cannot be spoken by the tongue—that
alone is God, not what people worship.

That which makes the mind think,
but which cannot be thought by the mind—that
alone is God, not what people worship.

That which makes the eye see, but which cannot
be seen by the eye—that alone is God, not what
people worship.

That which makes the ear hear, but which
cannot be heard by the ear—that alone is God,
not what people worship.

If you think that you know God, you know very
little, all that you can know are ideas and images
of God.
— The Upanishads

It is not easy to find happiness in ourselves, and it is not possible to find it elsewhere.
— Agnes Repplier

>︀︎⟋⟍

I learned this, that if you advance confidently in the direction of your dreams, and endeavor to live the life which you have imagined, you will meet with a success unexpected in common hours. You will put some things behind, you will pass an invisible boundary, new, universal, and more liberal laws will begin to establish themselves around and within you; or the old laws will be expanded, and interpreted in your favor in a more liberal sense, and you will live with the license of a higher order of beings.
— Henry David Thoreau

>︀︎⟋⟍

If you wish to travel far and fast, travel light. Take off all your envies, jealousies, unforgiveness, selfishness and fears.
— Glenn Clark

No amount of security is worth the suffering of a life lived chained to a routine that has killed your dreams.
— Kent Nerburn

Security is when everything is settled, when nothing can happen to you; security is the denial of life.
— Germaine Greer

The major value in life is not what you get. The major value in life is what you become. That is why I wish to pay fair price for every value. If I have to pay for it or earn it, that makes something of me. If I get it for free, that makes nothing of me.
— Jim Rohn

The secret of life is balance, and the absence of balance is life's destruction.
— Hazrat Inayat Khan

56

The self is one. Unmoving, it moves faster than the mind.
The senses lag, but Self runs ahead. Unmoving, it outruns pursuit.

Out of Self comes the breath that is the life of all things.
Unmoving, it moves; is far away, yet near; within all, outside all.
— The Upanishads

Transformation is a journey without a final destination.
— Marilyn Ferguson

People who say that life is not worthwhile are really saying that they themselves have no personal goals which are worthwhile. Get yourself a goal worth working for. Better still, get yourself a project. Always have something ahead of you to look forward to...to work for and hope for.
— Dr. Maxwell Maltz

Happiness is an attitude of mind, born of the simple determination to be happy under all outward circumstances.

Happiness lies not in things nor in outward attainments. It is the gold of our inner nature, buried beneath the mud of outward sense-cravings.
— J. Donald Walters

Life naturally evolves in the direction of happiness. We must constantly ask ourselves if what we are doing is going to make us, and those around us, happy. Because happiness is the ultimate goal. It is the goal of all other goals.

When we seek money, or a good relationship, or a great job, what we are really seeking is happiness. The mistake we make is not going for happiness first. If we did, everything else would follow.
— Deepak Chopra

Coincidences are God's way of staying anonymous.
— Unknown

58

The map is not the territory.
— Alfred Korzbyski

The best advice I can give is to ignore advice. Life is too short to be distracted by the opinions of others.
— Russel Edson

If you bring forth what is within you, what you bring forth will save you. If you do not bring forth what is within you, what you do not bring forth will destroy you.
— The Gospel of Thomas

You shall be free indeed when your days are not without a care nor your nights without a want and a grief.

But rather when these things girdle your life and yet you rise above them naked and unbound.
— Kahlil Gibran

Go as far as reason will take you,
then leap.
— Unknown

Live with intention. Walk to the edge. Listen
hard. Practice wellness. Play with abandon.
Laugh. Choose with no regret. Continue to
learn. Appreciate your friends. Do what you love.
Live as if this is all there is.
— Mary Anne Roadacher-Hershey

Perhaps, love is the process of my leading you
gently back to yourself.
— Antoine de St. Exupery

To love is to return to a home we never left, to
remember who we are.
— Sam Keen

It is not he who has lived the longest,
but he who has traveled the farthest, who knows
the most.
— Armenian Proverb

Ask the experienced rather than the learned.
— Arabic proverb

One of the saddest lines in the world is, 'Oh
come now—be realistic.' The best parts of this
world were not fashioned by those who were
realistic. They were fashioned by those who
dared to look hard at their wishes and gave them
horses to ride.
— Richard Nelson Bolles

As long as one keeps searching, the answers
come.
— Joan Baez

You tend to think of yourselves as a people of beginnings and endings. And yet, there is neither. That which you love will continue forever just as surely as that which you hate. Do away with that which you don't want by ceasing to hate and resist it. There is only one power and one force in the universe and I am that. I created you in my image and likeness so you are that.

The power to heal and prosper you, to guide and help you is not in the skies. It is and has always been within you. All you have to do is to become aware that I am there. There is mountain-moving power in each and every one of my children. You are a part of me and yet, at times, you think yourselves apart from me. You are made as I am. That which I do, you can also do. You are all co-creators with me.
— John Harricharan

That which you are seeking is causing you to seek.
— Uknown

Life is the ultimate I.Q. test.
— Alex Fraser

Life is a series of collisions with the future; it is not the sum of what we have been but what we yearn to be.
— Jose Ortega y Gasset

Life is what happens to you while you're busy making other plans.
— John Lennon

Life is not a spectacle or a feast;
it is a predicament.
— George Santayana

Learning is finding out what you already know.

Doing is demonstrating that you know it.

Teaching is reminding others that they know just as well as you.

You are all learners, doers, teachers.
— Richard Bach

>⌒⌒

. . . Life is the coexistence of all opposite values. Joy and sorrow, pleasure and pain, up and down, hot and cold, here and there, light and darkness, birth and death. All experience is by contrast, and one would be meaningless without the other.
. . . When there is a quiet reconciliation, an acceptance in our awareness of this lively coexistence of all opposite values, then automatically we become more and more nonjudgmental. The victor and the vanquished are seen as two poles of the same being. Nonjudgment leads to quieting of the internal dialogue, and this opens the doorway to creativity.
— Deepak Chopra

Treasure the love you receive above all. It will survive long after your gold and good health have vanished.
— Og Mandino

The power to stand alone is worth acquiring at the expense of much sorrowful solitude.
— George Bernard Shaw

You cannot be lonely if you like the person you're alone with.
— Wayne Dyer

There are many people who fear solitude, confusing it no doubt with loneliness. But in solitude, as nowhere else, there always is, or there may be, divine companionship.
— Archibald Rutledge

The vast majority of human beings dislike and even dread all notions with which they are not familiar. Hence it comes about, that at their first appearance, innovators have always been divided as fools and madmen.
— Aldous Huxley

><~

We don't see things as they are;
we see them as we are.
— Anaïs Nin

><~

Nature attains perfection, but a man never does. There is a perfect ant, a perfect bee, but man is perpetually unfinished. He is both an unfinished animal and an unfinished man. It is this incurable unfinishedness, which sets man apart from other living things for, in the attempt to finish himself, man becomes a creator. Moreover, the incurable unfinishedness keeps man perpetually immature, perpetually capable of learning and growth.
— Eric Hoffer

Dwell not on the past. Use it to illustrate a point, then leave it behind. Nothing really matters except what you do now in this instant of time. From this moment onwards you can be an entirely different person, filled with love and understanding, ready with an outstretched hand, uplifted and positive in every thought and deed.
— Eileen Cady

The only use of a knowledge of the past is to equip us for the present. No more deadly harm can be done to young minds than by depreciation of the present. The present contains all that there is. It is holy ground, for it is the past, and it is the future.
— Alfred North Whitehead

That's what learning is. You suddenly understand something you've understood all your life, but in a new way.
— Doris Lesing

God gave burdens, also shoulders.
— Yiddish Proverb

God created suffering so that we would learn to
help one another.
— Anita Bergen

Besides the noble art of getting things done,
there is the noble art of leaving things undone.
The wisdom of life consists in the elimination of
non-essentials.
— Lin Yutang

'Tis by no means the least of life's rules:
To let things alone.
— Balthasar Gracian

Change is created by those whose imaginations are bigger than their circumstances.
— Unknown

Even cowards can endure hardship; only the brave can endure suspense.
— Mignon McLaughlin

God bears with imperfect beings even when they resist His goodness. We ought to imitate this merciful patience and endurance. It is only imperfection that complains of what is imperfect. The more perfect we are, the more gentle and quiet we become toward the defects of other people.
— Unknown

A man is not finished when he is defeated. He is finished when he quits.
— Richard Nixon

If it's never our fault, we can't take responsibility for it. If we can't take responsibility for it, we'll always be its victim.
— Richard Bach

Keep away from people who try to belittle your ambitions. Small people always do that, but the really great make you feel that you, too, can become great.
— Mark Twain

Learn to say 'No'. It will be of more use to you than to be able to read Latin.
— Charles Haddon Spurgeon

The greatest discovery of my generation is that human beings can alter their lives by altering their attitudes of mind.
— William James

If you're going through hell, keep going.
— Winston Churchill

Cease trying to work everything out with your minds. It will get you nowhere. Live by intuition and inspiration and let your whole life be Revelation.
— Eileen Cady

Cherish your visions and your dreams as they are the children of your soul; the blueprint of your ultimate achievements.
— Unknown

71

Love has a bunch of keys
Under its arm.

Come, open the doors.
— Mevlana Lalaluddin Rumi

Love is the Law of God.
You live that you may learn to love.
You love that you may learn to live.
No other lesson is required of man.
— Mikhsil Naimy

To laugh often and love much, to win the respect
of intelligent persons and the affection of
children; to earn the approbation of honest
critics and to endure the betrayal of false friends;
to appreciate beauty; to find the best in others;
to give one's self; to leave the world a bit better,
whether by a healthy child, a garden patch or a
redeemed social condition; to have played and
laughed with enthusiasm and sung with
exultation; to know even one life has breathed
easier because you have lived, this is to have
succeeded.
— Ralph Waldo Emerson

Make it a rule of life never to regret and never look back. We all live in suspense, from day to day, from hour to hour; in other words, we are the hero of our own story.
— Mary McCarthy

I expect to pass through this world but once, any good thing, therefore that I can do, or any kindness that I can show to any fellow creature, let me do it now; let me not defer or neglect it, for I shall not pass this away again.
— Stephen Grellet

Of course, it's the same old story.
Truth usually is the same old story.
— Margaret Thatcher

I think that love is the only spiritual power that can overcome the self-centeredness that is inherent in being alive. Love is the thing that makes life possible or, indeed, tolerable.
— Arnold Toynbee

You change for two reasons: Either you learn enough that you want to, or you've been hurt enough that you have to.
— Anonymous

All this task and turmoil and noise and movement and desire is outside the veil; inside the veil is silence and calm and peace.
— Abu Yazid Al-Bismati

Don't wait until everything is just right. It will never be perfect. There will always be challenges, obstacles and less than perfect conditions. So what! Get started now. With each step you take, you will grow stronger and stronger, more and more skilled, more and more self-confident and more and more successful.
— Mark Victor Hansen

When you are inspired by some great purpose, some extraordinary project, all your thoughts break their bonds: Your mind transcends limitations, your consciousness expands in every direction, and you find yourself in a new, great, and wonderful world. Dormant forces, faculties and talents become alive, and you discover yourself to be a greater person by far than you ever dreamed yourself to be.
— Patanjali

Be the kind of person you would like to be with. Some people come into our lives, make footprints on our hearts and we are never the same. People are lonely because they build walls instead of bridges.
— Joseph F. Newton

There will always be times when you feel discouraged. I too have felt despair many times in my life, but I do not keep a chair for it; I will not entertain it. It is not allowed to eat from my plate. The reason is this: In my uttermost bones I know something, as do you. It is that there can be no despair when you remember why you came to Earth, who you serve, and who sent you here.
— Clarissa Pinkola Estes

Ask for what you want and be prepared to get it!
— Maya Angelou

The most beautiful people we have known are those who have known defeat, known suffering, known struggle, known loss, and have found their way out of the depths. These persons have an appreciation, a sensitivity and an understanding of life that fills them with compassion, gentleness, and a deep loving concern. Beautiful people do not just happen.
— Elizabeth Kubler-Ross

Happiness is to be found along the way, not at the end of the road, for then the journey is over and it is too late. Today, this hour, this minute is the day, the hour, the minute for each of us to sense the fact that life is good, with all of its trials and troubles, and perhaps more interesting because of them.
— Robert R. Updegraff

Experience taught me a few things. One is to listen to your gut, no matter how good something sounds on paper. The second is that you're generally better off sticking with what you know. And the third is that sometimes your best investments are the ones you don't make.
— Donald Trump

Success is the child of audacity.
— Benjamin Disraeli

The world ain't all sunshine and rainbows. It's a very mean and nasty place and I don't care how tough you are, it will beat you to your knees and keep you there permanently if you let it. You, me, or nobody is gonna hit as hard as life. But it ain't about how hard ya hit. It's about how hard you can get hit and keep moving forward.
— Rocky Balboa, *Rocky*

One of the most loving things you can do for another person is let them make their own mistakes, learn their own lessons and endure in the contrast of a life they don't really want. People only really change when they've hit rock bottom - sometimes the most loving thing you can do for a person is to let them and be there to help pick up the pieces. Permanent change comes from within, no one can give it to you.
— Jackson Kiddard

You cannot save people. You can only love them.
— Anaïs Nin

The four hardest tasks on earth are neither physical nor intellectual feats, but spiritual ones: To return love for hate; to include the excluded; to forgive without apology, and to be able to say 'I was wrong.'
— Unknown

Don't listen to those who say 'you're taking too big a chance.' Michelangelo would have painted the Sistine floor, and it would surely be rubbed out by today. Most important, don't listen when the little voice of fear inside you rears its ugly head and says 'they're all smarter than you out there. They're more talented, they're taller, blonder, prettier, luckier, and they have connections.' I firmly believe that if you follow a path that interests you, not to the exclusion of love, sensitivity, and cooperation with others, but with the strength of conviction that you can move others by your own efforts—and do not make success or failure the criteria by which you live—the chances are you'll be a person worthy of your own respects.
— Neil Simon

In life, finding a voice is speaking and living the truth. Each of you is an original. Each of you has a distinctive voice. When you find it, your story will be told. You will be heard.
— John Grisham

A roof to keep out the rain. Four walls to keep out the wind. Floors to keep out the cold. Yes, but home is more than that. It is the laugh of a baby, the song of a mother, the strength of a father. Warmth of loving hearts, light from happy eyes, kindness, loyalty, comradeship. Home is first school and first church for the young ones, where they learn what is right, what is good, and what is kind. Where they go for comfort when they are hurt or sick. Where joy is shared and sorrow eased. Where fathers and mothers are respected and loved. Where children are wanted. Where the simplest food is good enough for kings because it is earned. Where money is not so important as loving-kindness. Where even the teakettle sings from happiness. That is home. God bless it.
— Ernestine Schuman-Heink

I know for sure that what we dwell on is who we become.
— Oprah Winfrey

Not every sky will be blue and not every day is springtime. So on the spiritual path a person learns to find this kind of happiness without needing nice things to happen on the outside. Rather, you find happiness by being who you really are. This isn't mystical. Young children are happy being who they are. The trick is to regain such a state when you are grown and have seen the light and dark sides of life.
— Deepak Chopra

Fear is the cheapest room in the house.
I would like to see you living
In better conditions.
— Hafiz

Only one thing makes a dream impossible: the fear of failure.
— Paulo Coelho

Life and Other Options

Anita Bergen

84

About the Author

Anita Bergen takes joy in creating and editing books of all kinds, especially those that explore and express the spirituality in everyday life. Her best works are her quotation anthologies, which include *Life and Other Options* and *Pause and Reflect,* as well as several works in progress.

In addition to her talents with the written word, she is also a prize-winning artist and the former Vice President of Silvertech Industries, Inc. She has addressed numerous groups in locations such as Barcelona, Paris, London and Atlanta and remains an avid world traveler.

She continues writing and editing—with the help of the occasional swiping paw or curious, keyboard sniff from her four-legged menagerie— in suburban Atlanta, Georgia, USA.

Anita Bergen

Author's Note

It has taken countless hours of research and careful consideration to pick some of the best life-affirming, inspirational quotes to include in this volume.

Although literally millions of 'inspirational' thoughts have been spoken or written, a small number can be considered truly fantastic; many more are mediocre and some appear meaningless.

I've tried to the best of my ability to bring you only the 'best of the best' inspirational quotations and have credited the originators, as far as I can ascertain. Naturally, there are some quotations whose originators appeared as 'Anonymous' or 'Unknown.'

If you feel any quotation is incorrectly credited, I'd be grateful to make the appropriate corrections in future printings.

Send your comments to:

anita@inspirationonline.com

Anita Bergen